BE HEAL
JESUS' NAME

BE HEALED
IN JESUS' NAME

JOYCE
MEYER

WARNER
Faith®

NEW YORK BOSTON NASHVILLE

The advice herein is not intended to replace the services of trained health professionals, or be a substitute for medical advice. You are advised to consult with your health care professional with regard to matters relating to your health, and in particular regarding matters that may require diagnosis or medical attention.

All Scripture quotations, unless otherwise indicated, are taken from *The Amplified Bible* (AMP). *The Amplified Bible, Old Testament.* Copyright © 1965, 1987 by The Zondervan Corporation. *The Amplified New Testament,* copyright © 1954, 1958, 1987 by The Lockman Foundation. Used by permission.

Scripture quotations marked "KJV" are taken from the *King James Version* of the Bible.

Scripture quotations are italicized. Words emphasized by the author in Scripture quotations are set in italicized bold type. This emphasis does not appear in the original source of the Scripture quotation.

Warner Books Edition
Copyright © 2000 by Joyce Meyer
Life In The Word, Inc.
P.O. Box 655
Fenton, Missouri 63026
All rights reserved.

Warner Faith

Time Warner Book Group
1271 Avenue of the Americas, New York, NY 10020
Visit our Web site at www.twbookmark.com.

Warner Faith® and the Warner Faith logo are trademarks of Time Warner Book Group Inc.

Printed in the United States of America

First Warner Faith Edition: October 2002
10   9   8   7   6   5   4   3

ISBN: 0–446–69173–9
LCCN: 2002115779

Contents

❧

Contents

BE HEALED IN
JESUS' NAME

1

⟨❦⟩

RELEASING GOD'S POWER
TO HEAL

*M*any people believe God is **able** to heal them but aren't sure whether He **will** heal them. If you are one of those people, in this book you will find Scripture verses that reveal how willing God is to heal. You will also find an explanation of how to receive the healing God has for you according to the principles He gave us in the Bible.

Those principles may surprise you! They do **not** involve making yourself good enough to receive healing. God is a loving Father Who wants to do good things for His children. He wants to make us well.

If your child became sick and you had the ability to heal that child, you would do it. God is a much better parent than any of us could ever be. He wants to heal His children, and He has the ability to do it. He wants to do anything for us that will make our lives better.

Jesus said:

The thief (referring to Satan) *comes only in order to steal and kill and destroy. I came that they may have and enjoy life, and have it in abundance (to the full, till it overflows).*

John 10:10

First John 3:8 (KJV) tells us:

. . . For this purpose the Son of God was manifested, that he might destroy the works of the devil.

Jesus came to earth to destroy the works of the devil so that we *might have life,* and *have it more abundantly* (John 10:10 KJV).

Psalm 103 describes the benefits the loving Father has for His children. Verse 3 tells us one of those benefits is healing.

Bless (affectionately, gratefully praise) the
Lord, O my soul, and forget not [one of] all
His benefits—
Who forgives [every one of] all your iniquities,
Who heals [each one of] all your diseases,
Who redeems your life from the pit and
corruption, Who beautifies, dignifies, and crowns
you with loving-kindness and tender mercy;
Who satisfies your mouth [your necessity and
desire at your personal age and situation]
with good so that your youth, renewed, is like
the eagle's [strong, overcoming, soaring]!

Verses 2–5

Proverbs 4:20–22, one of the Scripture passages that reveals God's willingness to heal us, also contains one of the principles God gives us in His Word for receiving healing.

*My son, **attend to my words;** incline thine ear unto*
my sayings.

Let them not depart from thine eyes, keep them in the
midst of thine heart.

*For **they are life** unto those that find them,*
*and **health to all their flesh** (KJV).*

In Proverbs 4:20–22 Solomon is speaking of **God's** words, which we find in the Bible, "His Word." His words *unto those that find them* are *life* and *health to all their flesh!* (v. 22). *The Amplified Bible* includes the word "healing" in verse 22: *healing and health to all their flesh.*

According to *Strong's Exhaustive Concordance of the Bible* the Hebrew word translated "health" in verse 22 also means "a medicine."[1]

Exodus 15:26 says, . . . *I am the LORD that healeth thee* (KJV). Isaac Leesser translates this verse: . . . *I the Lord am thy physician.*[2] Psalm 107:20 (KJV) tells us: *He* (the Lord) *sent his word, and healed them, and delivered them from their destructions.*

The Lord is our Physician; the medicine He prescribes is His Word.

Because God's words are healing, or medicine, to those who find them, then a biblical principle to follow in order to receive healing is *attend* to God's *words*!

When you attend to something, you pay close attention to it. Learning the information in God's Word about His ability and willingness to heal and the methods He uses is similar to learning all you can about a doctor you are seeing for the first time.

You want to know that the doctor is qualified, experienced and capable of evaluating your health condition and prescribing the best treatment. The information you learn about the doctor gives you confidence to receive the advice and recommended treatment as the best approach for bringing the healing you need.

In the same way, to build confidence in God's willingness and ability to treat your condition, you learn about Him by reading His Word. When you attend to God's words on healing, you learn that God wants to do more than treat your condition—He wants to heal you completely!

We receive from God through faith. Mark 9:23 (NASB) tells us, . . . *All things are possible to him who believes.*

> *So then faith comes by hearing, and hearing by the word of God.*
>
> *Romans 10:17 NKJV*

Hearing God's Word on healing is important so that faith to receive the healing God has for you will come. But attending to God's words on healing is very important for another reason. The power to heal is actually inherent **in** God's Word. **It is the Word itself that heals you.**

God's Words Contain the Power to Heal

God's words, life unto those that find them (KJV) and healing and health to all their flesh (as we saw in Proverbs 4:22), are sharp and powerful! Hebrews 4:12 (KJV) tells us: *For the word of God is quick, and powerful, and sharper than any two-edged sword. . . .*

Jesus said, . . . *the words that I speak unto you, they are spirit, and they are life* (John 6:63 KJV). Jesus' words, recorded in the Bible, are Spirit and life. God's Word contains energy and ability!

Proverbs 18:21 tells us, *Death and life are in the power of the tongue. . . .* God's Word is a container for His power. When we activate His power by speaking His Word, His Word spoken out of our mouth contains power. Our words containing His power become like little bullets of *life* and *health* that shoot out into *all* our *flesh* to change our lives.

When I am teaching and speaking God's Word, it's as though I can see power in the words coming out of my mouth, carrying God's healing ability to the people in the congregation.

When that power begins to hit the people listening, they can bathe in it. They can be cleansed *by the washing of water with the Word* (Ephesians 5:26). And God's Word accomplishes what it is sent out to do.

Releasing God's Healing Through Speaking His Words

So shall My word be that goes forth out of My mouth: it shall not return to Me void [without producing any effect, useless], but it shall accomplish that which I please and purpose, and it shall prosper in the thing for which I sent it.

Isaiah 55:11

To learn the benefits God has made available to us, we attend to His Word by reading or hearing it. To bring into physical evidence the benefits we have learned are ours from His Word, we speak the Word in faith. And according to Isaiah 55:11 God's spoken Word does not return to Him void without prospering in the thing for which it was sent.

We release God's power to heal by speaking His Word with confidence in His ability and willingness to heal our condition.

2

꩜

GOD WANTS GOOD THINGS FOR HIS CHILDREN

*I*n order to have faith for something in any area, we must know it is God's will for the particular thing we are praying for to happen. We won't be able to use our faith to receive healing if we are not sure it is God's will.

In this section we look at the scriptural basis for believing that God wants each one of us to receive healing. It is important for us to understand that God as a Parent wants good things for His children. Matthew 7:11 (KJV) says:

If ye then, being evil, know how to give good gifts unto your children, **how much more shall your Father which is in heaven give good things to them that ask him?**

God wants to do good things for us because He loves us. We can **begin** to understand how much the Father loves us if we think about how much we love our children. However, God loves us because He **is** love. Love is not something He does; love is Who He is. (1 John 4:16.)

Love is all God knows how to do. And the Bible says, . . . *God is no respecter of persons* (Acts 10:34 KJV). He does not love one person more than He loves another one. He does not love the preacher at church more than He loves you, or the man working in the sound booth, or the piano player or the most prominent person you can think of. But sometimes we think that way—we think God loves other people more than He loves us!

God's love for us is complete, pure, steady, constant and unending. We can't be separated from it. (See Romans 8:38,39.)

God wants to have a personal relationship with us because, as a loving Father, there is so much He wants to do for us. He wants us to receive all the benefits He has for us that we read about in Psalm 103. To provide a Way for us to have a personal relationship with Him, God sent His Son, Jesus. Jesus said, . . . *"I am the way, and the truth, and the life; no one comes to the Father, but through Me"* (John 14:6 NASB).

We receive everything the Father has for us through Jesus: not only salvation—eternal life with the Father—but the benefits described in Psalm 103:2–5 and everything else.

> *In this was manifested **the love of God** toward us, because that **God sent his only begotten Son** into the world, **that we might live through him.***

> *1 John 4:9 KJV*

> *For **God so loved the world, that he gave his only begotten Son,** that **whosoever believeth in him** should not perish, **but have everlasting life.***

> *John 3:16 KJV*

The Scripture below shows us how much the Father wants to *freely give us all things.*

> *He that spared not his own Son, but delivered him up for us all, how shall he not with him also freely give us all things?*

> *Romans 8:32 KJV*

The problem is not on God's side—He is not withholding good things from us. The problem is on our side—not being able to receive what He has already made freely available for us. Many of us don't freely receive many, or any, of *all things* the Father has for us because we don't know they are available. Others of us who know what good things He has for us, don't know how to receive them.

First, to become an heir of God, of *all things* He has for us, we establish a personal relationship with Him by believing in His Son, Jesus. Galatians 3:26 (KJV) tells us: *For ye are all the children of God by faith in Christ Jesus.* And as a son (or child) of God, we become an heir of God, a fellow heir with Jesus. (See Romans 8:17, Galatians 4:7.)*

Also, to receive all the Father has for us, we must fully consider the great price Jesus paid for the purpose of making eternal life and all the other benefits freely available to us.

We saw in John 3:16 that whoever believes in God's Son will *have everlasting life.* And God wants all men to be saved—to receive everlasting, eternal life with Him.

*If you do not have a personal relationship with God, see the prayer at the end of this book to learn how to allow Him to come into your life.

Sozo: *Saved, to Be Made Whole*

The Greek word **sozo** is translated in some Scripture passages as "saved." **Sozo** is also translated in other passages as ". . . 'to make whole,' and, in the passive voice, 'to be made whole,' or 'to be whole. . . .' "[1]

In the two Scripture verses below, **sozo**, translated as "saved," describes receiving salvation through the Mediator between God and man, Jesus.

For this is good and acceptable in the sight of
God our Saviour;
*Who will have all men to be **saved**, and to*
come unto the knowledge of the truth.
For there is one God, and one mediator
between God and men, the man Christ Jesus.

I Timothy 2:3–5 KJV

That if thou shalt confess with thy mouth the Lord
Jesus, and shalt believe in thine heart
that God hath raised him from the dead, thou
*shalt be **saved**.*

*For with the heart man believeth unto
righteousness; and with the mouth confession
is made unto salvation.*

Romans 10:9,10 KJV

The same Greek word **sozo** is translated "whole" (as in deliverance "from sickness")—*"made . . . whole"*—in Matthew 9:22[2] (KJV) below.

*But Jesus turned him about, and when he saw her, he
said, Daughter, be of good comfort; thy faith hath
made thee **whole**. And the woman was made whole
from that hour.*

Jesus came not only to save us, but to make us whole in every way—to heal us. Do you see from the Scriptures we have looked at to this point how much God wants you to receive healing? He wants you to be completely made whole in **every** area of your life.

3

⁂

THE BASIS FOR
RECEIVING HEALING

*J*esus said:

*The Spirit of the Lord is upon me, because
he hath anointed me to preach the gospel to
the poor; he hath sent me to heal the brokenhearted, to preach deliverance to the captives,
and recovering of sight to the blind, to set at
liberty them that are bruised.*

Luke 4:18 KJV

Jesus continually healed people in His earthly ministry. In Matthew chapters 8 and 9, we read of Jesus healing person after person.

If you ever want to become encouraged concerning your healing, just open your Bible to Matthew chapters 8 and 9 and start reading. These two chapters contain one account after another of Jesus healing people who had diseases.

In this book we are establishing that it is God's will for people to be healed physically. There are many accounts in God's Word of the tremendous healings Jesus did, even bringing people back from the dead. Jesus also affirmed over and over that He came only to do the Father's will. (See John 6:38; John 5:19).

From the many accounts in the Bible of Jesus healing people and His statements that He came only to do the Father's will, we can see that it **is** God's will for people to be physically healed.

Healing Is God's Will

Hebrews 13:8 (KJV) tells us *Jesus Christ is the same yesterday, and to day, and for ever.* We can't say that healing passed away with the early church, which some people teach. What Jesus did in the days He was walking on the earth, He will also do for you today. If He was healing people then, He is certainly about the business of healing people today.

Isaiah 53 contains some of the most powerful teaching in God's Word on the subject of healing. *The Amplified Bible* makes the meaning of this passage crystal clear.

Verses 4 and 5 state:

Surely He has borne our griefs (sicknesses, weaknesses, and distresses) and carried our sorrows and pains [of punishment], yet we [ignorantly] considered Him stricken, smitten, and afflicted by God [as if with leprosy].

But He was wounded for our transgressions, He was bruised for our guilt and iniquities; the chastisement [needful to obtain] peace and well-being for us was upon Him, and with the stripes [that wounded] Him we are healed and made whole.

The word, "surely," that begins verse 4, doesn't leave any room for doubt.[1] *Surely He has borne our* ("our" means yours and my) *griefs (sicknesses, weaknesses, and distresses) and carried our sorrows and pains [of punishment]. . . .* The *New International Version* of the Bible words this portion of the verse, *Surely he took up our infirmities and carried our sorrows. . . .*

Verse 4 (AMP) continues:

> *. . . yet we [ignorantly] considered Him stricken, smitten, and afflicted by God. . . .*

One day as I was praying, God began to unfold to me a revelation about Isaiah 53:4,5. As I began to realize how many times we ignorantly consider Jesus—how many times we ignorantly consider what He **died** for us to have—I just began to weep.

Instead of seeing God as the Father Who loves us so much and wants to do so many things for us, many of us see Him through the eyes of religion. And "religion" does not always represent the good God the Scriptures reveal Him to be, the God I know, at all.

Jesus died, not because He was stricken and afflicted by God for something He did, but to take our sicknesses and diseases on His body so that we wouldn't have to experience those things.

Again Isaiah 53:5 (AMP) says:

. . . the chastisement [needful to obtain] peace and well-being for us was upon Him, and with the stripes [that wounded] Him we are healed and made whole.

Jesus died to bring us salvation, peace and healing.

As you read this, close your eyes for a moment after each description, and use your imagination. (God created your imagination to be holy and used for godly purposes.)

Before Jesus went to Calvary to be crucified on the cross, He was probably tied to some kind of a post, we believe, as was done before a Roman execution.[2]

In your imagination see Jesus tied to the post, and see a soldier, who is probably rather large, come out with a whip that has several strips of leather with little pieces of sharp bone and metal tied into each piece of leather.[3] See Jesus begin to receive those stripes that He took for the healing that you need.

One, two, three, four—He is probably starting to bleed, now—five, six, seven—I'm sure He's writhing in pain. Eight, nine, ten. . . The Romans didn't necessarily limit the number of stripes to the thirty-nine of Jewish law.[4] Jesus bore our sicknesses and diseases, taking them upon His own body, to the point, the Bible teaches, that He became totally unrecognizable. He wasn't even recognizable as a man. (See Isaiah 52:14 NIV.)

Jesus underwent that terrible persecution, humiliation and grueling beating, to the point of being unrecognizable as a man, then an excruciating, horrible death to take on our sin **and** to bear our sicknesses and diseases. He died not only for us to receive salvation—everlasting life with God through believing in Jesus—**but also** to provide healing for us.

The New Testament Scriptures below describe Jesus as fulfilling the prophecy of Isaiah 53 to provide **both** salvation and healing.

First Corinthians 15:3 tells us: . . . *Christ (the Messiah, the Anointed One) died for our sins in accordance with [what] the Scriptures [foretold]* (referring to Isaiah 53:5–12).[5] Jesus died to take on our sins so . . . *that whoever believes in him shall not perish but have eternal life* (John 3:16 NIV).

Matthew 8:16 states:

When evening came, they brought to Him
(Jesus) many who were under the power of
demons, and He drove out the spirits with a
word and restored to health all who were sick.

Verse 17, after describing the healings Jesus per-
formed in verse 16, tells us:

And thus He fulfilled what was spoken by the
prophet Isaiah. He Himself took [in order to
carry away] our weaknesses and infirmities and
bore away our diseases.

First Peter 2:24 (KJV) states that we were healed by
Jesus' stripes.

Who his own self bare our sins in his own body
on the tree, that we, being dead to sins, should
live unto righteousness: by whose stripes ye were
healed.

Jesus bore the stripes that were needful to obtain your healing. When you let a revelation of what Jesus did for you unfold to you, rather than concentrating on trying to figure out the answers to your problem, I believe that sickness and disease will not be able to remain attached to your body.

Fully consider the great price Jesus paid so that God could *freely give us all things,* and take hold of **all** the benefits available to you as a child and an heir of God.

God wants you to receive the healing you need. Take hold of your healing by faith.

4

❧

SIMPLE FAITH

*W*e receive healing in the same way we receive everything else from God: through faith. Paul's description of the Colossians' faith in Christ in *The Amplified Bible* is the best definition of faith I've ever heard: . . . *[that leaning of the entire human personality on Him* (described as God in Christ in Hebrews 6:12) *in absolute trust and confidence in His power, wisdom, and goodness]* (Colossians 2:5).

Faith Is Leaning on God

Having faith is not complicated. From Paul's definition we can see that faith is simply leaning on God in trust and confidence.

There is a little animal called a limpet that we can learn to be like in a way when it comes to leaning on God in simple faith. The limpet, a marine animal with a shell and a muscular foot, does one thing extremely well—it clings tightly to rocks.[1]

If you were walking along the seashore and approached a limpet on a rock without it sensing you were there, you could strike it with your walking stick, and it would fall.

A second limpet, further down on the same rock, sensing the danger would immediately react with its tremendous ability to cling. If you struck it, you wouldn't be able to knock it off the rock no matter how hard you tried, once it had begun to cling. That limpet wouldn't understand exactly what was happening—it wouldn't understand you, your walking stick or the intricate details of how God created its anatomy to work with the rock formation for the limpet's protection—it would simply do the one thing it knew how to do—cling!

In a similar way, you may not understand everything you would like to know about the doctrine of faith or exactly how God's words can be health or medicine to your flesh. But understanding those things is not a requirement for you to receive healing, or any of the other benefits, from God. God's requirement for you is simply this: Cling in faith to Jesus.

Use the Faith You Have

Sometimes people who want a healing more than anything are not sure they have enough faith to receive it. I want to encourage you that (as we saw before) Romans 10:17 tells us when we hear the Word of God, faith comes. If you have a personal relationship with God by believing in Jesus, God is in you through the power of the Holy Spirit. And where God is, there is faith. Romans 12:3 (KJV) tells us, . . . *God hath dealt to every man the measure of faith.* If God is in you, you already have faith!

When you hear the Word of God spoken and faith **comes**, I believe the *measure of faith* inside you rises up to meet the Word, and together they **go** out to do the job. Remember, it is the Word that heals you. When you speak God's words, they will *accomplish* and *prosper in the thing* they were sent to do (as we saw in Isaiah 55:11).

We see in the Scripture below that faith the size of a grain of a mustard seed is enough to move a mountain!

When Jesus' disciples asked Him why they were unable to cast out a demon:

> *He* [Jesus] *said to them, Because of the littleness of your faith [that is, your lack of firmly relying trust]. For truly I say to you, if you have faith [that is living] like a grain of mustard seed, you can say to this mountain, Move from here to yonder place, and it will move; and nothing will be impossible to you.*

> *Matthew 17:20*

People who are concerned that they don't have enough faith for healing need instead to turn their attention to learning how to use the faith they already have. Don't be concerned about whether your faith is perfect—release what you have and watch God work in your behalf.

Receive Healing as a Gift

Sometimes people want healing so badly that, without realizing it, they actually start **working** to try to **earn** it from God. They **try** to get enough faith to be healed instead of receiving healing from Him as one of the things He freely wants to give us.

You can't **earn** healing with great faith or anything else. You can't **buy** healing with your faith. Healing is not for sale. It has already been bought with the blood of Jesus. You can only **receive** healing with your faith. Faith is an avenue for receiving, not legal tender or money to use in buying something. There is a difference. Faith is a **gift** that is given to you, and you must receive it as a gift.

Romans 12:3 (kjv) tells us, . . . *God hath dealt to every man the measure of faith.* The *New International Version* words this verse as . . . *the measure of faith God has given you.*

I can well remember feeling condemned because I thought I did not have strong enough faith. If I prayed and did not get well right away, I began to receive Satan's lie that "I did not have enough faith."

One day I finally became tired of feeling condemned, and I said out loud as a declaration—"I have the amount

27

of faith I have, and I'm going to keep using what I have instead of worrying about what I don't have."

Believing is actually an act of the will, a decision, based upon what we have learned to be true about God. It is leaning on Him *in absolute trust and confidence* based upon our knowledge of how good He is and that He will do what He says in His Word.

We can **decide** to believe, then rest in the knowledge that the Word will *accomplish* and *prosper in the thing* it was sent to do. Real faith is a rest, not a struggle. Those who believe enter into the rest of God. (Hebrews 4:3.) It is wonderful to be in God's rest while we are waiting for the full manifestation of our healing.

Like the little limpet, cling to the rock. Cling to the Rock (1 Corinthians 10:4), Jesus, confidently waiting to receive what is rightfully yours as an heir of God through the blood Jesus shed to make it available for you.

Even now as I write this book, my husband, Dave, is waiting to see the manifestation of a physical healing that he needs and we are believing God for. He developed a blood clot in his leg and has been lying around for twelve days with his leg propped up. He is taking his medicine as the doctor recommended, but he is also taking the medicine of God's Word while steadfastly believing that God will completely remove the problem and that it will never return. Medicine usually treats symptoms; God's power removes the problem.

Dave is not frustrated or upset; he is in the rest of God because he is believing. He is not feeling condemned because he has not seen the full result yet. He is being thankful for each stage of progress, and he knows that . . . *God causes all things to work together for good to those who love God, to those who are called according to His purpose* (Romans 8:28 NASB).

Probably by the time you read this book, Dave will be completely well, but right now he is waiting just as you and many other people reading this book may be. We inherit the promises of God through faith and patience. (Hebrews 10:36.) There are times when we receive instant results from our prayers and other times when we must wait and be patient. It is not our responsibility to reason out "why and when"; we are to simply remain in childlike faith, knowing that our loving heavenly Father will always take good care of us and that it is impossible for Him to fail.

5

HINDRANCES TO HEALING

Our relationship with our heavenly Father is one of love. (See 1 John 4:16 KJV.) To receive from God, you must receive His love. You must believe that He loves you. And because He first loved us, we love Him back. (1 John 4:19.) Our loving Parent/child relationship with Him is similar to a loving parent/child relationship on earth. We relate to our heavenly Father by doing things pleasing to Him because we love Him.

He wants what is best for us. He wants us to walk in the Spirit—to live in a state of being open to Him, able to hear His voice—so that we will receive all He has for us in every area of life.

If we are intentionally living a life full of sin without any desire or attempt to stop, if we aren't seeking God to help us change, we are walking in the flesh. Just as a loving earthly parent will not give privileges to a child who is purposely belligerent, rebellious and disobedient, God will not give us privileges that will encourage us to walk in the flesh.

This does not mean that you must be doing everything perfectly for God to heal you. None of us is perfect in our performance. We can have a perfect heart toward God, a really sincere desire to do all things according to His will. According to Matthew 5:48 in *The Amplified Bible,* we grow into that perfection. The presence of the Holy Spirit inside of us makes us perfect in heart, but it takes some time for the flesh to get in line with the heart. We may make mistakes and do some things wrong, but God judges according to the heart. Understanding this will help you enter God's rest and receive all the good things He has for you.

Having something wrong in your life does not mean God will not heal you. But receiving *everything* God has for you—abundance in finances, divine health and in other areas of life—is based upon your relationship with your Father. Your heart must be right toward Him to receive from Him.

God wants your will to be in line with His will. He wants your thoughts to be in line with His thoughts as revealed in His Word. He wants your emotions to be under the control of the Holy Spirit.

Third John 2 tells us:

Beloved, I pray that you may prosper in every way and [that your body] may keep well, even as [I know] your soul keeps well and prospers.

If God is showing you something in your life that needs to be moved out of the way, He is not showing it to you to condemn you. He wants you to see how to operate differently in order to line up with His will so that you will be able to easily receive everything He has to give you.

God wants your soul—your mind, will and emotions— to prosper. Most of the time your physical man will not prosper beyond the level that your soulish man has prospered. God wants to be the Lord of the soulish realm as well as the spiritual and physical realm.

If you are full of bitterness, resentment and unforgiveness or have all kinds of open, known sin in your life and don't even care, in all probability you will not receive the physical healing you desire. But even though it is unlikely, God sometimes does perform a miracle, a healing, in a situation like this. Occasionally God will show Himself strong in someone's life in this way to demonstrate His love, to draw the person's attention to Him.

God wants to heal you, but He expects you to bring your soulish man in line with His Word. Spiritual maturity should be our #1 goal. It is even more important than our physical healing.

One of the greatest ways to clog up your pipe of faith, so to speak, is to have unforgiveness in your heart. You won't be able to receive very much from God if you are harboring unforgiveness, bitterness and resentment against someone else. The Bible clearly tells us that if we will not forgive other people of their sins, God will not forgive us. (See Mark 11:25,26 NASB.)

Matthew 9:2 gives an account of Jesus healing a paralytic, brought on a bed to Him. The first thing Jesus said to the paralytic was, . . . *your sins are forgiven you* (Matthew 9:2 NKJV). In this instance when the person was brought to Jesus for healing, He forgave the person's sins, and the paralytic was healed. (vv. 6,7.)

James 5:16 relates that we should confess our faults to be healed.

*Confess to one another therefore your faults
(your slips, your false steps, your offenses, your
sins) and pray [also] for one another, that you
may be healed and restored [to a spiritual tone
of mind and heart]. . . .*

The Scriptures show us how important it is to forgive. It would be a good idea to take a few steps back to make sure you aren't holding anything against anyone else, including anything that you may be angry at God about!

It is important that we keep sin out of our life, and God has provided the Way for us to keep our sins covered under the blood of Jesus through true, heartfelt repentance. (See Matthew 26:28.)

If you have sin in your life and you know it, you need to deal with it. Repent. Confess the sin. First John 1:9 (KJV) tells us: *If we confess our sins, he is faithful and just to forgive us our sins, and to cleanse us from all unrighteousness.*

Many people make sin much harder to deal with than it actually is by continuing to dwell on the sin after they repented and asked for forgiveness.

Sometimes people who know that God can heal them are not really sure He will. They look at themselves and think, *Am I too bad for God to heal?* Or they think they aren't as close to God or as "holy" as they think they need to be.

God understands where each of us is spiritually and emotionally, and He will meet us where we are if we will trust Him. Repent; accept forgiveness; turn from the sin and go on! God is faithful and just to forgive you and cleanse you from all unrighteousness. Then cling to Jesus in faith!

Unconfessed personal sin can be the root cause of sickness and disease, but that is not always the case. We live in a sinful world that is filled with germs and forces that break down our immune systems. Don't be too introspective, always trying to figure out what your sin is that caused you to have problems. Be open to God, do some soul searching, but don't go on a digging expedition that causes you to focus on yourself and everything that is wrong with you instead of focusing on Jesus and all that He is able to do for you.

As I have said before, if you have sinned, confess it, receive forgiveness and go on. If God shows you nothing in particular, then don't start imagining things. Stay in God's rest and hold fast your confession of faith in Him. I have discovered in my years of experience with God that He is well able to let me know loud and clear when I have displeased Him. I don't have to guess and get into reasoning to try to figure out why—I know!

There are times when other people can make us feel guilty and as if we must have done something wrong or we would not be having the problems we are having. I can remember one time in particular when one of our children got into some pretty serious trouble. The questions that friends were asking Dave and me definitely indicated that they were searching for what Dave and I had not done right as parents that caused the child to behave this way.

One of his teachers even asked him if he thought he got into trouble because Dave and I traveled in ministry and were not home with him all the time. They wanted to know if he felt loved and cared for. He promptly told them that He loved us very much and we loved him very much and that he got into trouble because he made wrong choices, not because we traveled.

Obviously, if we had not been maintaining a right relationship with him, that could have been the root of his problem, but my point is that people often jump to conclusions and say things that can make us feel guilty and condemned. It is always best to listen to God and not necessarily to people when it comes to finding out what the root cause of your problem is. The truth was, we had worked very hard in our life to make sure we kept a right relationship with our children and that they knew they were very important to us.

There have been times when I was sick and people actually said to me, "You must have sin in your life or this would not be happening," and, "Something must be wrong or you would be receiving your healing!" These same people had a totally different attitude later in life when they became sick and did not find answers to their situation immediately. It is very easy to judge people and say hurtful things when we have not experienced what they are going through. I always find mercy to be more powerful than judgment.

Misconceptions That Prevent Healing

Many religious doctrines, traditions of thinking contrary to the truth of God's Word, and misconceptions are taught that have kept people from receiving healing from God. We saw that without an understanding of the cleansing power of God's forgiveness, some people think they are too bad for God to heal.

Others have been taught that God gives us sickness in order to teach us something. Stopping to consider what it actually means for God to be our loving Parent, as we have done in this book, will help people realize that teaching isn't true.

For example, no loving parent would teach a two- or three-year-old baby not to play with fire on the stove by putting the child's hand in the fire! In the same way God does not teach us things by making us sick. Yes, God corrects us, but He does it as our loving Parent. (Proverbs 3:12.)

God knows how to correct me when I get out of line and need to be corrected, and He also knows how to correct you. He doesn't have to do it by whipping up a little cancer or a little arthritis or a car wreck to throw on us!

If you are a parent, how do you treat and teach your children whom you love so much? To teach your children to look for cars before crossing a street, would you put your children in the middle of the road, then have a car run over them? You wouldn't do anything like that to teach your children something! And God, your loving Father, won't do anything like that to you to teach you something, either!

Hebrews 12:9 states that God is *the Father of spirits*. He deals with us on a spiritual level. God is the Father of my spirit, and you probably feel the same way I do if you've ever been "spanked" in the spirit by God—I would rather be sick in my flesh any day of the week than to be "sick" in my spirit.

If it is true that God puts sickness on you to teach you something, or that it is God's will for you to be sick on occasion, then you would be out of God's will by taking an aspirin, going to the doctor or doing anything else to recover from a sickness. You would be out of God's will to attend any meeting that had prayer for the sick because you might receive a healing when it was God's will for you to be sick.

If it is God's will for you to be sick so that He can teach you something, the best thing you can do if you are sick is to lie down and get as sick as possible!

When you look at this tradition of teaching in this way, the teaching doesn't make sense! But there are literally thousands of Christians who are held captive in that area because they have been taught that sickness is God's will. That teaching has convinced them that we can glorify God by suffering and being patient in sickness. If that doctrine is true, then Jesus robbed God of a great deal of glory when He healed so many sick people who were suffering!

Tradition says the age of miracles has passed away. Once when I was preparing to teach, God impressed something upon me as I was praying. He said, "Tell them not only has the age of miracles not passed away, but I have not even begun yet."

God is going forward, not backward! If the early church needed the miracle-working power of God, how much more do we need it today? Some of the traditions people are taught and the beliefs they hold as a result are foolish. But often those people have believed the teaching for so long, they have never thought to carefully examine the doctrines to determine if they are true!

Tradition says that it is God's will to heal some people, but not all. If that were true, how could you have faith to be healed if you had to first find out if you were one of the favored ones whom God had selected to heal?

. . . *God is no respecter of persons* (Acts 10:34 KJV). His will is healing and wholeness. His timing and methods may be different in every case, but His will remains the same. Knowing this is the major key to trusting God all the way through and continuing to stand on His Word.

Joy and peace are found in believing. (Romans 15:13 KJV.) Doubt and unbelief only make us more miserable. When Abraham had no human reason to hope, he hoped on in faith. (Romans 4:18.) We can rejoice in our hope; we can believe for change. All the while we stay positive that the power of God's Word is working in our bodies, bringing them to a place of strength and health.

Job's Afflictions and Paul's Thorn

People often ask questions about two accounts given in the Bible concerning healing: "Why was Job afflicted?" and "Why did the apostle Paul suffer with a thorn in the flesh?"

Job 1:1–2:8 gives the account of the series of sudden, devastating tragedies, including an affliction of boils which covered his entire body, that overcame Job, a godly man of great wealth.

Setting Your Standard

Job 1:4,5 gives us insight that Job often operated out of fear rather than faith. Job's sons held feasts in honor of each other's birthdays. After the period of feasting was completed, Job sent for his sons and had them purified. He also offered burnt offerings early in the morning to God for each son. Job was afraid that his sons might have sinned.

Concerning other circumstances, Job stated: *For the thing which I greatly fear comes upon me, and that of which I am afraid befalls me* (Job 3:25).

Job had a powerful relationship with God and knew better than to operate in fear. But Job was operating in fear instead of faith, and that fear opened the door for Satan to attack him.

God gives us principles to operate within for our own good and protection. When we operate outside of those principles, we are moving into an area that has opened a door for Satan to enter. And in that area, there may be little God can do to protect us at the time.

The Lord later . . . *turned the captivity of Job and restored his fortunes. . .* and. . . *gave Job twice as much as he had before* (Job 42:10). But the losses and afflictions Job experienced before then were so devastating that Job wished he had never been born. (Job 3:3.)

Second Corinthians 12:7 refers to Paul's *thorn in the flesh* which Paul describes as *the messenger of Satan to buffet me.*

> *And lest I should be exalted above measure*
> *through the abundance of the revelations,*
> *there was given to me a thorn in the flesh, the*
> *messenger of Satan to buffet me, lest I should*
> *be exalted above measure (KJV).*

Much has been written about the identity of Paul's thorn.

"The thorn was designated as a 'messenger of Satan,' perhaps to indicate that Satan, as an adversary, resisted Paul's ministry. . . .the thorn may refer to some physical infirmity. . . ." or ". . . to some painful experience which was spiritual in nature, such as temptation or the opposition of the Jews."[1]

It may have been ". . . some great trouble or some great temptation. . . ." or ". . . the indignities done him by the false apostles, and the opposition he met with from them. . . ."[2]

No matter what Paul's thorn was, when it comes to healing, the identity of Paul's thorn doesn't really matter. The answer to the questions "Why was Job afflicted?" and "Why did the apostle Paul suffer with a thorn in the flesh?" is simply this: Neither Paul nor Job is your standard.

Jesus Is Your Standard

Let us believe we can have what Jesus had, not what Paul or Job had. Jesus walked in divine health, and that should be our goal.

If you feel that you can never reach a level higher than the one Job, Paul or other great people of faith reached, you are looking at people as your standard instead of Jesus. You are interpreting Romans 8:17 to read:

*And if we are [His] children, then we are [His] heirs also: heirs of God and fellow heirs [or joint-heirs, KJV] with . . . **Job** . . . or . . . with **Paul** . . . !*

The standard God gave us is this: *fellow heirs [or joint-heirs, KJV]* with Christ!

Joint-Heirs with Jesus

Everything that belongs to the Father belongs to Jesus. (John 17:10 NASB.) Hebrews 1:2 tells us that God appointed His Son *Heir and lawful Owner of all* things.

Everything God has for you, He gives to you because you are a joint-heir with Jesus Christ. You have a right to everything Jesus has!

By believing that you can have everything Jesus has, you are looking at the standard God wants for you. *We must keep fixing our eyes on Jesus, the author and perfecter of faith . . .* (Hebrews 12:2 NASB).

Many times we have a tendency to look at ourselves or circumstances instead of looking at God. We need to keep fixing our eyes on Jesus and looking at what God said He can and will do.

Why Don't Some People Receive Healing?

If a healing that was desired and prayed for does not happen, we may or may not ever learn the reason. The Bible says *our knowledge is fragmentary*—we know *in part* (1 Corinthians 13:9,12).

We don't know everything there is to know. But instead of focusing on what we don't know by trying to find a reason that, in many cases, can't be determined, we need to focus and build our faith on the truth we *do* know: what the Bible teaches about healing.

We don't have all the answers, but we can reach the point of realizing we don't have to know them all, as long as we know the One Who does. There is a tremendous rest that comes with realizing that we don't have to understand everything that happens.

I used to allow myself to become confused if someone I knew who was believing God for healing did not receive it. Sometimes the person was me, and other times it was someone else. I finally learned through years of experience that I needed to trust God even in things I could not mentally understand.

I have prayed many times and received healing, but at other times I had to walk through a sickness. Sometimes I have received healing quickly, and other times I have had to wait much longer than I would have liked to. I have seen people who were absolute skeptics concerning the doctrine of supernatural healing receive great miracles, and yet others who seemed to have all the faith in the world have remained sick or even died.

I don't have all those answers, but I made up my mind that according to God's Word physical healing is part of our inheritance, and I am going to keep believing and stay away from reasoning . . . *that sets itself up against the [true] knowledge of God* . . . (2 Corinthians 10:5). I may need to go to the doctor, but I am still believing God. I may have to wait and go through some things, but I am still going to believe God's Word and stand in faith that I will have a complete victory in God's timing, however He chooses to minister to me.

Don't allow yourself to become confused; just keep believing. Jesus told Mary and Martha in John 11:40 that if they would keep on believing, they would see the glory of God. Often we must "keep on believing" for a while before we see a breakthrough.

God Is Working for Us

And so faith, hope, love abide. . . .

1 Corinthians 13:13

It is a tremendous comfort to know that even though we don't always understand why some things happen, we have faith, hope, and we know that God loves us.

We also know that the Lord is good (Psalm 106:1; 107:1; 118:1,29; 136:1) and that He, with power (as described in Ephesians 1:19–22 NASB) of *surpassing greatness* that He has *toward us who believe,* the *mighty power* (KJV) that raised Christ *from the dead, and seated Him at His right hand in the heavenly places, far above . . . every name that is named* and *put all things in subjection under His feet. . .* (NASB) is working for us!

. . . If God is for us, who can be against us?

Romans 8:31 NIV

For the eyes of the LORD run to and fro throughout the whole earth, to show Himself strong on behalf of those whose heart is loyal to Him. . . .

2 Chronicles 16.9 NKJV

Keep your eyes on your standard, Jesus, with Whom—as a child of God—you are joint-heir, to receive the healing God has for you.

6

⊛⊙⊛

METHODS GOD USES
TO HEAL

God has provided many ways for you to receive your healing.

One of the nine *spiritual gifts (the special endowments of supernatural energy)* (1 Corinthians 12:1) God works in men by the Holy Spirit (vv. 6,11 NIV) is *the gifts of healing* (v. 9 KJV). Notice that the word "gifts" is plural. Healing can come in many ways.

Sometimes people receive an instantaneous visible change in their body that comes through the "power" and "inherent ability"[1] of a miracle. This is another of the nine spiritual gifts in operation, *the working of miracles* (v. 10). The word *miracles* in this verse "is used of works of a supernatural origin and character, such as could not be produced by natural agents and means."[2]

Sometimes people receive miracles from God, but most of the time people receive healing from Him as part of a process. The meaning of the word *healing* in verse 9 is "a cure."[3]

God heals many people, and the visible change comes as a result of the process which takes time. In fact after you receive prayer, many times you won't notice any immediate difference physically. You may not feel any better. You might even feel worse!

My husband provided an example that gives a clear picture of how it is that we can feel worse after healing has begun. If I fell down the steps one night and skinned my knee, my knee would hurt much worse the next morning after it started to heal than immediately after I fell.

After you pray or receive prayer for healing and you don't notice any immediate physical difference, just know this means that the healing power is working in your body. Concentrate on taking the medicine your Physician prescribed, by attending to His Word on healing.

If a doctor prescribed medicine for you, you would probably expect to take the whole bottle, and possibly a refill, before you experienced or saw complete results. You wouldn't throw the bottle away if you didn't feel one hundred percent healthy after taking one spoonful or pill!

After praying for healing, at least give God the same opportunity as you would a bottle of medicine! Keep taking your medicine, the Word, and continue *leaning* on God in *absolute trust and confidence* (Colossians 2:5).

Attending to God's Words

Whether your visible healing comes through a process or you receive a miracle, it is important to know how to attend to God's words. If you receive a miracle, you need to know how to keep it!

Some people lose the miracles they receive in healing meetings because they go home without knowing what to do to keep them. They need to know how to attend to God's words. As we saw, Proverbs 4:20,21 tells us to incline our ears to God's sayings, to let them not depart from our eyes and to keep them in the midst of our heart. Joshua 1:8 tells us to meditate on the Word.

We can attend to God's Word through hearing, reading and speaking it. You may want to listen to teaching tapes on healing or listen over and over to healing Scriptures on tape. It's a good idea, also, to read the healing Scriptures aloud yourself. You may want to buy a couple of good books on healing. Meditate on Isaiah chapter 53 to gain an understanding of what Jesus did to obtain healing for us. Then, **simply believe!**

They **Shall** *Recover*

Mark 16:17,18 describes a method God uses to heal, the laying on of hands, one of the signs that will follow those who believe. This Scripture shows us the confidence we can have in knowing the healing power is working in our bodies after we receive prayer for our healing. It tells us that once hands are laid on the sick, they *shall* recover.

> *And these signs shall follow them that believe; In my name . . . they shall lay hands on the sick, and they shall recover (KJV).*

Verse 18 is worded . . . *they shall recover,* not "they *may* recover" or "it is *hoped* they will recover." If you feel worse after God's Word was prayed for your healing, whether laying on of hands was used or another of God's methods, keep your confidence in Isaiah 55:11. When God's Word is spoken it *shall accomplish* and *prosper in the thing* for which it was sent. In James 5:14,15 (below) we read of other methods God uses to heal.

The Lord Will Restore the Sick

Is anyone among you sick? He should call in the church elders (the spiritual guides). And they should pray over him, anointing him with oil in the Lord's name.

And the prayer [that is] of faith will save him who is sick, and the Lord will restore him; and if he has committed sins, he will be forgiven.

Notice that James chapter 5 instructs those who are sick to seek prayer. For God to include this instruction in the Bible is another strong indication of His willingness to heal!

In Bible times the sick called for the elders in the church to pray for them. We can understand the term "elders" to refer to the spiritually mature. If you are in a situation in which you are sick but are unable to locate someone who functions under the title of "elder," this verse does not mean you should go without prayer. If I feel sick, many times I ask my husband, who is spiritually mature, to pray. Call for someone whom you believe has the faith to pray for you. Be anointed with oil, pray the prayer of faith in the Lord's name and you will be restored.

> . . . *The earnest (heartfelt, continued) prayer*
> *of a righteous man makes tremendous power*
> *available [dynamic in its working].*

James 5:16

In Matthew 8:5–8,13 we read of another way God heals. A centurion asked Jesus to heal his servant boy, who was lying at the centurion's house . . . *paralyzed and distressed with intense pains* (v. 6).

The centurion said to Jesus:

> . . . *but only speak the word, and my servant boy will*
> *be cured* (v. 8).

*Then to the centurion Jesus said, Go; it shall
be done for you as you have believed. And the
servant boy was restored to health at that very
moment (v. 13).*

As did the centurion, we can take hold by faith of the
inherent power to heal in the Word of God!

God's Mighty Power

Sometimes God's power is so strong, standing up in its
presence is hard!

First Kings 7:51–8:11 tells us that after Solomon completed his work in building the house of the Lord and the
ark of the Lord was brought in, a cloud, the glory of the
Lord, filled the Lord's house, *So the priests could not stand
to minister because of the cloud. . .* (8:11).

When Paul, formerly Saul, was converted on the road
to Damascus . . . *suddenly there shined round about him
a light from heaven: And he fell to the earth . . .* (Acts 9:3,
4 KJV).

Sometimes in healing meetings, people who receive
prayer fall over on the floor. We call this being slain in the

Spirit, slain in the power of God. This is what happened to the priests and Paul in the Scriptures above.

Receiving your healing doesn't have one thing to do with whether you're slain in the Spirit. If you're the only one in a prayer line of people who isn't slain in the Spirit, Satan will try to get you to occupy your mind with trying to figure out why you weren't. Some people aren't slain in the Spirit because of their type of personality.

Remember, God is a Father and loves us. He doesn't do things to scare or hurt us.

God's Power Is in Jesus' Name

Philippians 2:9,10 (NIV) states:

*Therefore God exalted him [Jesus] to the
highest place and gave **him the name that is
above every name,**
that **at the name of Jesus** every knee should bow,
in **heaven** and on **earth** and **under the earth.***

Have you ever noticed that everything in this world has a name? Trees, people, bugs, buildings, streets, all our foods and all diseases have names. The name of Jesus is **above** every other name, and it contains so much more power than everything else in existence that every knee must bow to it and submit to its authority in all three realms—heaven, earth and under the earth.

Jesus Christ is:

*Far **above** all rule and authority and power and dominion and **every name that is named** [above every title that can be conferred], not only in this age and in this world, but also in the age and the world which are to come.*

Ephesians 1:21

There is more power in the name of Jesus than there is power in the name of cancer or in the name of a tumor, arthritis or heart disease. And God has given us use of that powerful name.[4] Jesus said:

If you ask anything in My name, I will do it.

John 14:14 NKJV

First John 5:14,15 (NASB) tells us:

*And this is the confidence which we have
before Him, that, if we ask anything according
to His will, He hears us.
And if we know that He hears us in whatever
we ask, we know that we have the requests
which we have asked from Him.*

We have seen that healing is God's will. And anything in God's will we ask for in Jesus' name, we will have the requests for which we asked.

If you are sick, it is God's will for you to be well. Speak the healing Scriptures in the name of Jesus, which is more powerful than anything else that exists, to that sickness, believing you are healed. Believe the sickness or disease will submit to the authority of Jesus' name.

7

⤜⧚⤛

FAITH AND PATIENCE
BRING GOD'S PROMISES

*W*hen you've filled yourself up with the Word, or attended a series of healing meetings or a conference, it's easy to have full confidence that you've been healed when you haven't yet seen a change physically. But one morning when you wake up and you don't feel any better, you may be tempted to decide to give up. It is vital to receiving or maintaining your healing that you apply the principles taught in Hebrews 10:35,36 and Hebrews 6:11,12.

Hebrews 10:35,36:

Do not, therefore, fling away your fearless confidence, for it carries a great and glorious compensation of reward.

*For you have need of steadfast patience and
endurance, so that you may perform and fully
accomplish the will of God, and thus receive
and carry away [and enjoy to the full] what is
promised.*

One of the biggest problems people in the body of
Christ are having today is flinging away their confidence
before they *receive and carry away [and enjoy to the full] what
is promised.*

One time when I was ministering to a woman in a
meeting I was holding, I was suddenly impressed with a
picture of her traveling down a road. When she was halfway
to her destination, she turned around and returned to the
starting point. Then she started off again and did the same
thing: halfway down the road, she turned around and went
back to the starting point.

Many people in the body of Christ do this very thing!
They go halfway down the road to healing, then give up,
fling away their confidence and go all the way back to the
start!

Second Corinthians 5:7 (NIV) tells us, *We live by faith,
not by sight.* Because we are called to live a life of faith, not

feeling, we are to trust what the Word tells us, not in what we feel or don't feel.

If you are like me, there are times when you don't feel saved. But even when you don't feel saved, you still are. It's the same with your healing. You may not feel healed, but you are healed. The healing power of God is residing in your spirit.

Hebrews chapter 6 tells us to *imitate those who through faith and patience inherit the promises* (v. 12 NKJV).

> *But we do [strongly and earnestly] desire for each*
> *of you to show the same diligence and sincerity*
> ***[all the way through]** in realizing and enjoying*
> *the full assurance and development of [your] hope*
> ***until the end.** In order that you may not grow*
> *disinterested and become [spiritual] sluggards, but*
> *imitators, behaving as do those who **through faith***
> ***(by their leaning** of the entire personality **on God***
> ***in Christ in** absolute **trust and confidence** in*
> *His power, wisdom, and goodness) **and by practice***
> ***of patient endurance and waiting are [now]***
> ***inheriting the promises.***

Hebrews 6:11,12

When you wake up that morning not feeling any better, you can decide to fling away your confidence that you have received your healing. Or you can decide to continue to lean on God in confidence and patience, resting in the knowledge that the great reward confidence carries is yours: receiving and carrying away and enjoying to the full what is promised.

God wants us to be diligent to practice *patient endurance and waiting* in order to inherit the promises. And everyone wants to be able to carry away to the full what is promised. Keeping fearless confidence for healing when you don't see any physical improvement, and may even feel worse, is not easy. The Bible doesn't tell us the way will be easy, but it does tell us that God will show us **the Way**.

Psalm 34:19 tells us that many evils confront the righteous, . . . *but the Lord* (the Waymaker) *delivers him out of them **all***. John 16:33 tells us we can be of good cheer because Jesus has overcome the world. Jesus said, . . . *[I have deprived it of power to harm you and have conquered it for you.]*

With the Waymaker inside us, . . . *we are more than conquerors and gain a surpassing victory through Him Who loved us* (Romans 8:37). Believing these truths will give you confidence. Before we ever encounter a problem we can have confidence that we already have *surpassing victory* in it through Jesus.

The answer to the question, "Do you want to be an overcomer?" is usually, "Yes!" The answer to the question, "Do you want something to overcome?" is usually, "No!"

We want to be overcomers, but many of us don't want to encounter anything that we will need to overcome!

We must expect that problems to overcome will come our way. And in many cases overcoming them will be hard! But God will make us able. People who run from the hard places in life will spend their entire lives running. And they will run around and around the same mountains instead of making progress. It will take years for them to experience victory over something they could have dealt with fairly quickly if they had stopped running and faced it.

To receive the fullness of the promise you desire from the Lord, the healing you desire, you must be diligent to lean on Him in confidence *all the way through* to the finish. Hebrews 6:12 warns: *In order that you may not grow disinterested and become [spiritual] sluggards. . . .*

Proverbs tells us that the lazy sluggard will not prosper in life. *The soul of a lazy man desires, and has nothing; but the soul of the diligent shall be made rich* (Proverbs 13:4 NKJV). The sluggard, too lazy to plow in the winter because of the cold, begs for food during harvest time because he has nothing. (20:4 AMP, KJV.) Because he sleeps too much, poverty will come on him. (6:10,11.)

God does not want us to be lazy because He wants us to receive everything He has for us. And to do that we must be diligent. Many people haven't yet realized that overcoming hard things can be fun. God put His Spirit inside of us so we would be ready for every challenge.

When you reach the point of not shrinking back from the hard places, you will begin to soar like an eagle over the mountains that come into your life. I've gone *all the way through* some hard times in my life and *through faith and patience* I'm now *inheriting the promises* in those areas.

Face the problem that needs to be overcome, and be diligent to go all the way through to the finish so that you will enjoy to the full the promise on the other side.

Conclusion

❧

To live in the divine good health God has for you, keep the following points in mind.

First, Jesus bought healing for you with His blood. Healing is yours as a gift. You receive it with your faith. You can't buy or earn it.

Second, it is illegal for Satan to put sickness on you, but he will if you let him.

It was illegal for Satan to kill Jesus, but he was able to do it because Jesus let him. Jesus let him because He had a good reason—He was going to use Satan's illegal action to redeem the world!

It is important for you to understand that it is illegal for Satan to put sickness on you, and there is no good reason to let him do it.

Resist sickness and disease in the same way you resist the temptation to sin. Sickness doesn't come on you all of a sudden. You begin to feel little indications that you are getting sick. When those indications first come, your responsibility as a believer is to resist those at that time.

If a temptation came to me to go out with a man other than my husband, I would resist that with everything in me because I know I'm not going to do something like that. We need to resist sickness and disease with the same godly indignation because it's illegal for Satan to put sickness on us.

Third, it is important to continually speak the Word of God on healing in Jesus' name to our bodies. The water of the Word (Ephesians 5:26) that is alive, sharp and powerful (Hebrews 4:12 AMP) will continually wash our bodies to keep them free from disease.

Prayer to Receive Healing

Pray the following aloud.

Father:

I thank You for sending Jesus to die on the cross to provide salvation and healing for me. I thank You for the use of Jesus' name which is more powerful than any other name that exists. The name of Jesus is above the name of (<u>name of sickness or disease</u>) that is in my body illegally. In the authority and power of Jesus' name, that (<u>name of sickness or disease</u>) must leave my body.

According to Proverbs 4:20–22, Your words are health to my flesh, and according to Isaiah 55:11, Your spoken Word will accomplish and prosper in the thing it was sent to do. I speak that, in Jesus' name, by Jesus' stripes I am healed according to 1 Peter 2:24, and I believe that I receive my healing. I thank

You that as my Father You love me and have provided
healing for me as part of my inheritance. In Jesus'
name, amen.

Healing Scriptures to Confess

Now confess out loud the following Scriptures—do so as
often as you need strength and encouragement. Confess
the Scriptures so that they apply to you. For example speak
1 Peter 2:24 (below) over yourself by saying, ". . . by His
stripes I was healed. . . ."

Who his own self bare our sins in his own body
on the tree, that we, being dead to sins, should
live unto righteousness: by whose stripes ye were
healed.

1 Peter 2:24 KJV

Beloved, I pray that you may prosper in every
way and [that your body] may keep well, even as
[I know] your soul keeps well and prospers.

3 John 2

Surely He has borne our griefs (sicknesses, weaknesses, and distresses) and carried our sorrows and pains [of punishment], yet we [ignorantly] considered Him stricken, smitten, and afflicted by God [as if with leprosy]. But He was wounded for our transgressions, He was bruised for our guilt and iniquities, the chastisement [needful to obtain] peace and well-being for us was upon Him, and with the stripes [that wounded] Him we are healed and made whole.

Isaiah 53:4,5

My son, attend to my words; consent and submit to my sayings.

Let them not depart from your sight, keep them in the center of your heart.

For they are life unto those who find them, healing and health to all their flesh.

Proverbs 4:20–22

Bless (affectionately, gratefully praise) the
Lord, O my soul; and all that is [deepest]
within me, bless His holy name!
Bless (affectionately, gratefully praise) the
lord, O my soul, and forget not [one of] all
His benefits—
Who forgives [every one of] all your iniquities,
Who heals [each one of] all your diseases.

Psalm 103:1–3

He sends forth His Word and heals them and
rescues them from the pit and destruction.

Psalm 107:20

Saying, If you will diligently hearken to the
voice of the Lord your God and will do what is
right in His sight, and will listen to and obey His
commandments and keep all His statutes, I will
put none of the diseases upon you which I
brought upon the Egyptians, for I am the Lord
Who heals you.

Exodus 15:26

*And He went about all Galilee, teaching in
their synagogues and preaching the good news
(Gospel) of the kingdom, and healing every
disease and every weakness and infirmity
among the people.*

*So the report of Him spread throughout all Syria,
and they brought Him all who were sick, those
afflicted with various diseases and torments,
those under the power of demons, and epileptics,
and paralyzed people, and He healed them.*

Matthew 4:23,24

*And thus He fulfilled what was spoken by the
prophet Isaiah. He Himself took [in order to
carry away] our weaknesses and infirmities and
bore away our diseases.*

Matthew 8:17

*And behold, a woman who had suffered
from a flow of blood for twelve years came
up behind Him and touched the fringe of
His garment;*

*For she kept saying to herself, If I only touch
His garment, I shall be restored to health.
Jesus turned around and, seeing her, He said,
Take courage, daughter! Your faith has made
you well. And at once the woman was restored
to health.*

Matthew 9:20–22

*And these attesting signs will accompany those
who believe: in my name they will drive out
demons, they will speak in new languages;
They will pick up serpents; and [even] if they
drink anything deadly, it will not hurt them;
they will lay their hands on the sick, and they
will get well.*

Mark 16:17,18

Is anyone among you sick? He should call in the church elders (the spiritual guides). And they should pray over him, anointing him with oil in the Lord's name.

And the prayer [that is] of faith will save him who is sick, and the Lord will restore him; and if he has committed sins, he will be forgiven. Confess to one another therefore your faults (your slips, your false steps, your offenses, your sins) and pray [also] for one another, that you may be healed and restored [to a spiritual tone of mind and heart].

The earnest (heartfelt, continued) prayer of a righteous man makes tremendous power available [dynamic in its working].

James 5:14–16

Prayer for a Personal Relationship with the Lord

❧

God wants you to receive His free gift of salvation. Jesus wants to save you and fill you with the Holy Spirit more than anything. If you have never invited Jesus, the Prince of Peace, the Healer, to be your Lord and Savior, I invite you to do so now. Pray the following prayer, and if you are really sincere about it, you will experience a new life in Christ.

Father,

> *You loved the world so much, You gave Your only begotten Son to die for our sins so that whoever believes in Him will not perish, but have eternal life.*

Your Word says we are saved by grace through faith as a gift from You. There is nothing we can do to earn salvation.

I believe and confess with my mouth that Jesus Christ is Your Son, the Savior of the world. I believe He died on the cross for me and bore all of my sins, paying the price for them. I believe in my heart that You raised Jesus from the dead.

I ask You to forgive my sins. I confess Jesus as my Lord. According to Your Word, I am saved and will spend eternity with You! Thank You, Father. I am so grateful! In Jesus' name, amen.

See John 3:16; Ephesians 2:8,9; Romans 10:9,10; 1 Corinthians 15:3,4; 1 John 1:9; 4:14–16; 5:1,12,13.

ENDNOTES

Chapter I

1. James E. Strong, "Hebrew and Chaldee Dictionary," in *Strong's Exhaustive Concordance of the Bible* (Nashville: Abingdon, 1890), p. 73, entry #4832, s.v. "health," Proverbs 4:22: ". . . properly, *curative,* i.e. literally (concretely) a *medicine,* or (abstractly) a *cure;* figuratively (concretely) *deliverance,* or (abstractly) *placidity. . . .*" (Abbreviations have been spelled out in this and in all other endnotes from Strong.)

2. Isaac Leesser, *Twenty-Four Books of the Holy Scriptures Carefully Translated After the Best Jewish Authorities* (New York: Hebrew Publishing Company, n.d.), p. 115.

Chapter 2

1. Strong, "Greek Dictionary of the New Testament," p. 70, entry #4982, s.v. "saved," 1 Timothy 2:4, Romans 10:9; "whole," Matthew 9:22.

W.E. Vine, *Vine's Complete Expository Dictionary of Old and New Testament Words* (Nashville: Thomas Nelson Inc., 1984), "An Expository Dictionary of New Testament Words," p. 674, s.v. "WHOLE (made), WHOLLY, WHOLESOME," B. Verbs. 2. "*sozo* . . . e.g., *Matt. 9:21, 22* (twice). . . ."

2. Vine, "New Testament Words," p. 547, s.v. "SAVE, SAVING," A. Verbs. 1. "*sozo* (. . . 4982), 'to save,' is used (as with the noun *soteria,* 'salvation,') (a) of material and temporal *deliverance* from danger, suffering, etc. e.g . . . *from sickness, Matt. 9:22,* 'made . . . whole' (RV marg., 'saved') . . . (b) of the spiritual and eternal salvation granted immediately by God to those who believe on the Lord Jesus Christ, e.g., . . . 1 Tim. 2:4."

Chapter 3

1. Strong, "Hebrew Dictionary," p. 12, entry #403, s.v. "surely," Isaiah 53:4: "*firmly;* figuratively, *surely;* also (adversely) *but:*—but, certainly, nevertheless, surely, truly, verily."

2. William D. Edwards, MD; Wesley J. Gabel, MDiv; Floyd E. Hosmer, MS, AMI, "On the Physical Death of Jesus Christ," *JAMA, The Journal of the American Medical Association* (March 21, 1986), Vol. 255, no. 11, p. 1457.

3. *JAMA,* p. 1457.

4. *JAMA,* p. 1458.

Also, *Matthew Henry's Commentary on the Whole Bible: New Modern Edition,* "Isaiah 53:4–9, The Humiliation of the Messiah," Electronic Database, copyright © 1991 by Hendrickson Publishers, Inc. Used by permission. All rights reserved.

5. Cross reference for 1 Corinthians 15:3 per NASB (1960, 1962, 1963, 1968, 1971) and AMP.

Chapter 4

1. *The American Heritage® Dictionary of the English Language, Third Edition,* copyright © 1992 by Houghton Mifflin Company, s.v. "limpet." Electronic version licensed from InfoSoft International, Inc. All rights reserved. And *The Concise Columbia Encyclopedia,* licensed from Columbia University Press, copyright © 1995 by Columbia University Press, s.v. "limpet." All rights reserved.

Chapter 5

1. Nelson's *Illustrated Bible Dictionary,* copyright © 1986 by Thomas Nelson Publishers, s.v. "Thorn in the Flesh." All rights reserved. Used by permission.

2. *Matthew Henry's Commentary,* s.v. "2 Corinthians 12:1–10." Used by permission. All rights reserved.

Chapter 6

1. Vine, "New Testament Words," p. 412, s.v. "miracles," 1 Corinthians 12:10.

2. Vine, "miracles.'

3. Strong, "Greek Dictionary," p. 37, entry #2386, s.v. "healing," 1 Corinthians 12:9: "a cure (the effect):—healing." From p. 37, entry #2390 ". . . to *cure* (literally or figuratively):—heal, make whole."

4. My teaching, "His Glorious Name," (available on audio-cassette and videotape) contains detailed information on this subject.

References

Some Scripture quotations are taken from the *New American Standard Bible®*, (NASB®) Copyright © The Lockman Foundation 1960, 1962, 1963, 1968, 1971, 1972, 1973, 1975, 1977, 1995. Used by permission.

Scripture quotations marked "NIV" are taken from the *Holy Bible, New International Version®*. NIV®. Copyright © 1973, 1978, 1984 by International Bible Society. Used by permission of Zondervan Publishing House. All rights reserved.

Scripture quotations marked "NKJV" are taken from the *New King James Version*. Copyright © 1982 by Thomas Nelson, Inc. Used by permission. All rights reserved.

About the Author

Joyce Meyer has been teaching the Word of God since 1976 and in full-time ministry since 1980. She is the bestselling author of more than sixty inspirational books, including *In Pursuit of Peace, How to Hear from God, Knowing God Intimately*, and *Battlefield of the Mind*. She has also released thousands of teaching cassettes and a complete video library. Joyce's *Enjoying Everyday Life* radio and television programs are broadcast around the world, and she travels extensively conducting conferences. Joyce and her husband, Dave, are the parents of four grown children and make their home in St. Louis, Missouri.

To contact the author write:

Joyce Meyer Ministries
P.O. Box 655
Fenton, Missouri 63026
or call: (636) 349–0303
Internet Address: www.joycemeyer.org

*Please include your testimony or help
received from this book when you write.
Your prayer requests are welcome.*

To contact the author
in Canada, please write:
Joyce Meyer Ministries Canada, Inc.
Lambeth Box 1300
London, ON N6P 1T5
or call: (636) 349–0303

In Australia, please write:
Joyce Meyer Ministries-Australia
Locked Bag 77
Mansfield Delivery Centre
Queensland 4122
or call: 07 3349 1200

In England, please write:
Joyce Meyer Ministries
P.O. Box 1549
Windsor
SL4 1GT
or call: (0) 1753–831102

Joyce Meyer Titles

Managing Your Emotions
Healing the Brokenhearted
Me and My Big Mouth!
Me and My Big Mouth! Study Guide
Prepare to Prosper
Do It Afraid!
Expect a Move of God in Your Life…Suddenly!
Enjoying Where You Are on the Way to Where You Are Going
The Most Important Decision You Will Ever Make
When, God, When?
Why, God, Why?
The Word, the Name, the Blood
Battlefield of the Mind
Battlefield of the Mind Study Guide
Tell Them I Love Them
Peace
The Root of Rejection
If Not for the Grace of God
If Not for the Grace of God Study Guide

JOYCE MEYER SPANISH TITLES
Las Siete Cosas Que Te Roban el Gozo
(Seven Things That Steal Your Joy)
Empezando Tu Día Bien (Starting Your Day Right)

BY DAVE MEYER
Life Lines